"Jennifer Wallace's *Raising the Sparks* is an extremely powerful garland of poems, filled with earned Ignatian discernment and the rabbinic wisdom of the Kabbalah's *tikkun olam,* once more igniting those sparks from the Original Creation and splintering of the Lord's Big Bang in our common fall from grace to a return—step by amazing step—to learning how to pay attention to the infinite grace abounding around us. There's an honesty and wit in these poems that echo and play contrabasso with Merton and Hopkins, and especially with Berryman's late *Addresses to the Lord,* a yearning for the Mystical that—if you listen closely enough—will stagger you."

—**Paul Mariani,** author of *The Mystery of It All: The Vocation of Poetry in the Twilight of Modernity*

"Jennifer Wallace's *Raising the Sparks* peers into the intimate moments of Life to reveal its wondrous and mysterious unfolding. Each poem takes you into a world that at first seems to belong to another and then makes itself known as your own. A book to be savored."

—**Rabbi Rami Shapiro,** author of *Accidental Grace*

"There is a deep intimacy, a buck-naked honesty, shot through the prayer poems (or is it poem prayers?) of Jennifer Wallace's latest collection, *Raising the Sparks,* a title that takes its name from 16th-century mystical Judaism's telling of the sacred story of the 'shattering of vessels,' in which our holy purpose is to repair the world through the gathering up of divine sparks scattered and strewn in time's beginning when God's presence could not be contained. But it is in the epistolary section, 'Letters to Jesus,' where it's as if we've entered the holy of holies of some anchoress-poet's cell, and we can only hope that our prayer might catch the slipstream of hers, so beautifully wrought, so chiseled to the bone is each blessed utterance. Poetry or prayer, Wallace makes me reach to catch her rising sparks."

—**Barbara Mahany,** author of *Slowing Time, Motherprayer,* and *The Stillness of Winter*

"*Paraclete* in Hebrew has had several meanings, chief of them I believe is "one who consoles." This may even be the metaphoric meaning of *Raising the Sparks*, the beautiful new book by Jennifer Wallace. I have known her meditative poems since before her earliest collection; her poems have steadily grown in their mystical power and philosophic approach to seeking consolation for herself and for others. There are many different paths to wisdom and many ways to structure a parable or a prayer; almost all of them can be found in this heartfelt book, whether the kerruling gulls of nature or the carved whale of a man named Homer (really)."

—**Michael Salcman**, author of *Shades & Graces: New Poems*,
inaugural winner of the Daniel Hoffman Legacy Book Prize,
and *Necessary Speech: New & Selected Poems*

"Jennifer Wallace's honest and perceptive poetry is rooted in earthy 'leafcrunch and mudslip' of the quotidian, yet unerringly finds 'a deeper gravity' which draws us into another country altogether. *Raising the Sparks* is 'alive with uncertain certainty,' shot through with gleams of both reluctance and faith. These poems resist 'kneel[ing] in the fire that burns for you,' but all the while glitter with 'this burning, uninvited,' throwing sparks which summon us to see 'an optimism in the crooked distance.'"

—**Laura Reece Hogan**, author of *Litany of Flights: Poems*

RAISING

Poems

THE

Jennifer Wallace

SPARKS

IRON
PEN

PARACLETE PRESS
BREWSTER, MASSACHUSETTS

2022 First Printing

Raising the Sparks: Poems

Copyright © 2022 by Jennifer Wallace

ISBN 978-1-64060-511-4

The Iron Pen name and logo are trademarks of Paraclete Press.

Library of Congress Cataloging-in-Publication Data

Names: Wallace, Jennifer, 1954- author.
Title: Raising the sparks / Jennifer Wallace.
Description: Brewster, Massachusetts : Iron Pen/Paraclete Press, 2022. |
    Summary: "In these poems, Wallace endeavors to find God in all things,
    and elevate them to holiness"-- Provided by publisher.
Identifiers: LCCN 2021037348 (print) | LCCN 2021037349 (ebook) | ISBN
    9781640605114 | ISBN 9781640605152 (epub) | ISBN 9781640605138 (pdf)
Subjects: LCGFT: Poetry.
Classification: LCC PS3573.A4263 R35 2022 (print) | LCC PS3573.A4263
    (ebook) | DDC 811/.54--dc23
LC record available at https://lccn.loc.gov/2021037348
LC ebook record available at https://lccn.loc.gov/2021037349

10 9 8 7 6 5 4 3 2 1

Published by Paraclete Press
Brewster, Massachusetts
www.paracletepress.com

Digitally printed

We must learn to live in the world.
Robert Penn Warren

CONTENTS

LAMENTS AND BENEDICTIONS

LETTERS TO JESUS†

RAISING THE SPARKS‡

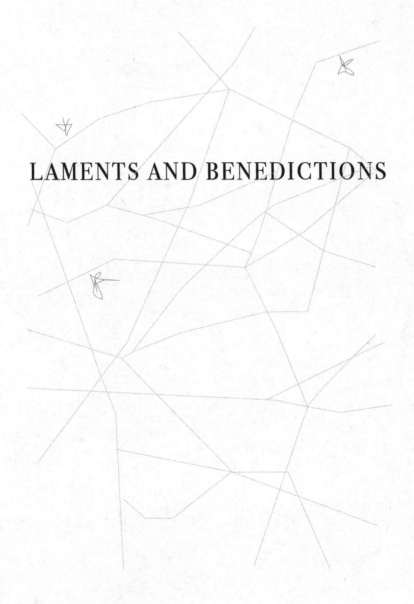

LAMENTS AND BENEDICTIONS

To All of You, Who Are Out There

Your beingness energizes me.

Though we might not have met, I can
picture you — out in the fields, studios, cubicles,
in your living rooms, libraries, among the scrap heaps.
Maybe in your pick-up truck, hospital bed. Maybe
you are folding your monogrammed towel.

Surely, I expect, you wonder and worry.
I bet you're alive with uncertain certainty.

We are kin — attuned, beads in the one web,
likewise set aglitter by the same shining star.

And, if you believe all this, you're as gullible as me
or as wishful, eternally scanning the heart's horizons.

This is my wager, my reach, my offering, my handshake;
right here, in your hands, your ear, wherever and
      whenever you are.

The Man Billions Pray With
—for Pope Francis

He prays, too — on his balcony, alone in his room;
    white robes rest in holy cabinets
    far from his puffed-up cardinals, arms crossed at the gates.

When he takes off his velvet shoes at night,
switches off the lights, we are alike.
It's not blasphemous to say so: mistaken, grievous,
we are both alone in our separate quarters,
the suffering cross ever-hanging on the wall about our hearts.

We want the same peace for the same 'turning world,'
for the lonely souls we call our own.

Bad News Soon Becomes Normal Days

All of what was planned has been released or hijacked.
Who knows which, or by whom?

An aviary door, wrenched open; every cherished being
freely flying out of reach, out of sight, giving way,
    over and over
to whatever the sky happens to be on each new day.

They come home at nightfall, roost out of sight, only
to leave again at dawn. Every day — revised —
and waiting to be revised again.

We continue with our planning —
all our crumpled lists end with the same words:
"Come back! Come back! We've stockpiled the oily sunflower,
millet, your favorite — cracked corn."

A Poem for Those Who Suffer, Sent Out to all Their Angels

Please watch out for them in their clutch of sadness.
Slide your warmth — cloud-soft — under their heads.

And the ones who care for them, also help *them*.

City Bus

A stubbled man unweighted himself
on the city bus today. Easily. Let go.
His arm tight against mine. He slept,
head flopped on my shoulder in a soft pile.

"Hmm," I wondered. Push him aside? Shrug him off?
Help him to my lap — so high, after shooting up?
So tired after working all night?

I was there with him,
all the while wondering. And finally,
I let it all be fine.

It was a good day, to have started this way.
On the bus, he and I.

In Dark Winter

— *for Katherine Kavanaugh*

In dark winter
ink-stained morning equals ink-stained night.
The numb sun, if it appears, hardly shines —
brittle in the birdless wind.

In dark winter
the day slips early away,
an orange-pink splits the shrouded sky,
but briefly, before a blue-black violet muffles again.

The wood I've hauled makes a trail inside,
bark and ice chips on the rug. Messy wild.
Once the stove door shuts, all goes quiet — even flames.
The cottage windows, sealed tight, stare at me and I stare at them.

In this artic season, far from dormant,
insight is old and filled with ghosts:
    Orion's child broods with the Dane upon the ramparts;
    the frozen match girl huddles near the bricks with her
            frozen gloves;
    fugitives from inner realms bed down in their heart caves,
            alert to the howling wolves.

A household lit at the horizon's edge
recedes further and further recedes.
Without light's sharp resolution,
a deeper gravity pulls everything
toward nearness and
"other than" becomes "the same."

And I reside inside, imagining what was
before the famous breathing into clay,
temptation, trees or names; before
the Lord said anything about light.

In this muted clarity, dark meets dark.
Minor chords resound. A pressing need
unfolds 'the maker's holy hands.'
And I, yet formed, am zero — warming at the hearth of faith.

Lament

Each day the papers have more to say
about those among us (among *us!*),
who shoot, stab, spit at others,
even though the ones they target
are mostly like themselves.

Haters love their sons and daughters,
their gods and rivers, eagles, lizards, leaders, too.
They are like us, but
on a rampage, tipping the funeral stones.
Fearmongers stir up trouble.
We must live again with water hoses,
bullet hoses, attack dogs, attack slogans.

In this scary season,
on the ropes in one giant ring,
look at mercy stumble —
neglected in its corner —
within reach, but weak.
Who among us will intervene?

Paradox

— after a sculpture by Scottish artist Steve Dilworth

Feather made of stone,
a thing that lifts and also fails to lift.
Nothing quite works: air argues with earth,
earth with air. Angels battle rock, rock longs for heaven.

Like objects in a mirror,
but with a second, facing mirror.
Never ending, nowhere to land. Wide moiré mesh —

onward, sideways and back again.

And isn't that just the way it is —
even our failures meet the infinite.

Light Litany

The world upside downs itself
with awful notions. People
who hate people seem to be in charge.

When, for a flash, we unplug the news,
we feel the feelings underneath our thoughts
and government becomes a new name for trauma.
A person can sink deep, morass.

What *is* that urge that often comes? To find and not give up?
To say yes instead of no?
If Cohen was right, and the light — no matter what — gets in,
if our 'long loving looks at the real' do not cripple us,
if pockets are emptied for all our neighbors
and helping becomes our new language, then,

what would be released would be
a flock of doves, each with two wings.

What would be true would be two new words:
"me and you," "you and me."

Yesterday the Cat Got a Dove

It looked almost gone, so I covered it with a trash bag
and went indoors to wait it out. Later, I returned to see — thinking
I would whack it with a shovel, a mercy killing.
I almost didn't lift the plastic,
but at the last minute thought I should. And off it flew
to the garage roof where, if birds could, it crouched down.

A second dove came to keep watch over it.
After ten minutes of small waddles on the roof's steep peak,
a thunderstorm approached. Heavy rains and big enough winds
to knock little things off their feet. After the storm passed, I
    looked again;
both birds were gone.

This morning only one dove is perched there.
Oh, you expected something different?

Bad Times and Their Causes

— S. A. Andrée (failed Artic balloonist)

Will we forever search outside ourselves for
    what might explain

why   the gene breaks
why   the commander drops the bombs
        the home burns
        the legacy stings?

Why do crops fail, the calf refuses to be born?
Why do the addict's bottle and needle go one way and not
    the other?

Inheritance?
A roll of sinister dice?
Mistakes unapologized for?

Some of it belongs to its owners, their explanations
    dodge the point.
The knot resists solution.
Tangles get further tangled
        regardless/because of all our thought.

Too bad. That's that. Move on.

Meditation on a Photograph of a Manta Ray
— for Jann Rosen-Queralt

Look at you here: unmoving, unnatural in my hands.
The photograph gives you voice —

We speak one word: *"looking-at-you-looking-at-me."*

I want to drop my landed pretenses and slide into the frame,
into your salty, cobalt skies, where I might be decreased under
   your flexing wing.

We speak the same word: *"looking-at-you-looking-at-me."*

How close you come with your bold, quiet eye —
I shudder to think what you think of me.

What secrets do you shelter? Please, something other than
your awful gasping in the nets. What ancient learning will
   you share?

We speak the same word: *"looking-at-you-looking-at-me."*

Bird-fish, fish-bird — cloak me that I may be freed,
from my parasitic ambitions, my naïve beliefs that I might
   create a better sea.

When I turn this page, return me to myself,
made softer, restless for the newness of our peace.

We speak the same word: *"seeing-you-seeing-me."*

Body of Water

Held by two shores or by ten.
By a cobalt pitcher. Held by skin.

The stuff is shapeshifter —
salt, brackish, mud-laced delta, crystal springs
urging up from the deep down, from the thinnest places,
from holy wells — where the saints of Ireland
found their wildest dreams, where normal people
go to keep their hair from falling out.

It offers a warm bath for neurons fired by ideas.
An internal river made of molecular attraction;
Three atoms bind and become, make a tree tick,
a muscle heave. It fuels the poet's genius so he can call it,
'…the medium for an anemone to dream.'

The minister plunges one body into another.
One of us snickers, another offers praise.

Our large star works its magic
and waters yield to clouds,
vapors of a northern season slip ghostly
in encounter with the last remaining warmth of summer ponds.

And once the season turns, under the Arctic's breath,
it will seize up and fall
as piles of glorious diamonds.

An aging human gazing out
will reach into the freezer for a dozen cubes of ice
and use them to squelch the fire in her shoulder
made from shoveling way too much.

Snowed In

The winter sky has fallen knee-deep
and the only "going" is from the woodstove to the chair.

Too deep for the dog to do its business; the poor thing
attempts a small, cleared patch we've opened near the door
but decides to use the rug instead.

The storm is a miracle; touchable atmosphere.
What might be called inconvenient, is now
a flood of crystals gathered in a shovel or a glove, or
glittery drifting whaleish bodies rolling over each other below
    the pines.

School's closed, workplace locked, car wedged between
    towering mounds.
A landscape — so slow to change — transformed in half a day.

Pull on the heavy boots; go out to play.
What is found out there? A house-dwelling human set free
as if in the salty ocean, learning again the ways to move,
    to breathe.
A doorway to the 'other world' under the one we thought
    we knew.

Sleeping with a River under Me

A full day on the water, digging in against a stiff wind.
The river was not our friend. Likewise the wind.
Muscle ache, argument.

We could hardly notice the limestone cliffs
with their ancient shells embedded long ago
before the seas became the river that carved
and bent its shores. So far back, beyond
what we could fathom, while on vacation
during which we existed mostly in our complaints.

During the wakeful night, 33 degrees,
and grumbling in the small tent,
I woke from a dream — uncushioned yet floating,
buoyant, rocking with the river under me.

How strange, with all the thoughts that could compete,
the one I noticed was comfort — not solid, but uncertain.
Sleeping with a river under me.

The Effort

—for Dana Rosenstein

1.

Not the thing (things) that happened
   but what didn't happen after.

And so, on her own. Without.
Again and again.
A little kid, fresh from the bath,
   had been.

2.

Some part of her hid a box without knowing.
Deeper and deeper in her chest.
Other parts in there, carrying all of it.
Unable to do harm, but harmful.
The worst part, out of reach, not what happened —
   not the splitting, scattering —
   but the gasp, shudder. Where the clock stopped.

It is still there, the box. Core. Atomic.
"Forsaken" is packed in there
   where a heart would beat if it were whole.

3.

So, that's it, right?
Discovered.
Live with it, right?
A little kid without.
No.

A little kid with a dark bottomless box
  where love would be, where the warped treasure
  protects by warping.

4.

But guess what?
The room where stuff happened,
  in the house of negligence —
    the bed is made
    the faceless faces wander now almost without consequence.
Because the lights are on
  and the "empty" that was there, the substance of absence —
    that's gone.
The lights are on. There's no "there" there.
I turned them on. Someone helped me —
  my very own Virgil
  swaddled, labored, led and loved.
And the "not" disappeared,
  washed in deep breathing, lungs unclenched, unfisted heart
  a homeless soul, now lit — which is grace,
  which is courage, substance that is presence.

5.

My Virgil handed me the cord: "Something awful happened.
  It's no longer happening.
Look, here's the light."

"Ok," I said. "I'll believe you.
I'm turning it on. I believe you."

6.

Again and again.

There is another world, and it is under this one
    —Paul Éluard

A world folded like a pocket map or origami frog,
tucked in a crack in the world's stone wall
or sewn into the lining of an old woolen coat.

The gods of this place have not been born yet. Nor the sun,
nor the stars, nor the void between them. No oceans, rivers,
forests, sand grains glittering. No blabbermouths, bullies
nor any silent cloistered types. No colors, music,
no poets, especially.
All the various histories do not apply.

The world under this one would be free of all the stories and any
    imaginings.
A world unable to consider me. What a tragedy!

The War Shadow

The war shadow hung over the meadow,
bubbled up from under the stones.

Our people hung their people in the summer nights.
The thick air fit close, insect clicks made odd music.
Someone planted a fire tree for light.

It was not the first time: the turning and returning.
We are still living it down.

On the Occasion of Pittsburgh's Synagogue Massacre

I should not have been born American, child of post-war
    affluence rising.

My heart is with Poland, with Europe's yellow-starred families
    torn from their roots.
I don't deserve their fear, their suffering, their courage — it is
    theirs.
But the long-gone Führer's logo painted yesterday on their
    worship house?
I can't stomach the killings, the mocking salutes.

I'm with Celan, whose mother's blond hair turned ashen.
I'm with Osip, 'forged and pacing, forged and laboring
in horizonless Voronezh's asylum eye.'

Here I am in my warm house, my pantry filled with bread;
with Yehuda, I 'console myself with short breaths.'

What can I do? Having only my brief encounter
    with their words?
which I will not burn,
thousands of psalms floating like their courage
in the frightening skies.

Dark Trio & Coda

Sharp blue day.

Inside the body: dull, after fighting.

Above the lake, an osprey.
Wild hunting: five times, five different times of day.

I say to myself: "Stay sharp."
I say: "Stay open. Damn it, fist,
open!"

Not sure of much except
a boulder rolled over trust.

"It's all in the mind," they say.

My mind is all I have.

In the textured forest:
something golden in the depths —
an optimism in the crooked distance.

And to get there: up and over the slick rocks,
the cracked branches,
the leaf-covered pit left by the storm-toppled oak.

Coda —
After disaster: an odd gleaming.

Easter Vigil

There will be other mornings like this,
lit by a stone's scrape. And in that place,
the answers get up and walk; their reasons
heaped in piles where they were left.

Forget the tea and cakes. Consolation equals
the drift of continents. Other theories, uncomposed.
We can be almost sure of some forgiving latitude —
April will arrive because the planet tilts and turns.

Dogwood buds, magnolia — all scent and flesh —
will resurrect from winter's hardpack. Granite
will be here until it flakes to sand. But the mind
resists its species and wrestles with heaven's flimsy nest.

In Jerusalem, the three faiths come and never go.
If evidence exists, it must be in attempts to show it's so.

An Ecology, Earth Day 2020

—for Suzanne Garrigues

From the porch corner, a perfect rabbit scanned the front yard.
Black marble eye — intense. Curved backbone — tense.
Alert-in-its-nose, and ears twitching. "What color?," R. asked.

"Rabbit color," I said, because how can I describe
from inside the house, the multiple strands, shades
and tones of so many hairs? "Overall, brown."

A weak, pedestrian response. Typically human,
typically inadequate. And when a warbler flock
flittered in to feed on the gnats, and the northwest

wind gusted with unexpected cold, and the autumn
pinecones dropped for squirrels and chippers to find,
I put down my pen and wondered. Everything

made sense, even as the inevitable eagle swooped by.

Unintentional Beauty

We called it "beautiful," the photo I made as a record
of what was: atmosphere, the day's new light.

I wasn't aiming for anything I knew of, but
the late moon, not yet set, entered from behind the clouds,
just like that — shot through my eyes and into my heart's
    soft spot.

I didn't set the arrow, didn't pull the string.
The moon couldn't help it.
A combination of elements "did their thing."
I was among them. I received the gift.

When the Trees Sing

Early morning.
The treetops' cheeping, trilling, squawking, chirping
carried me back to the cusp of reason, to a time
when untroubled confidence enabled such wild pleasures as —
"Listen! Listen, the trees are singing!"
Not a time for, "No, that can't be true," but a time
for a naïve tuning of ourselves to possibilities
made real by an unverified authority residing in our hearts.

Close your eyes. Can you hear them now?
What do you think, how do you feel
as you give voice to their mesmerizing names?

Pawpaw
Possomhaw
Loblolly
Boxelder
Tupelo
Baldcypress
Sweetgum
Holly
Overcup Oak.

*Praise restores us to the world again, to our
luckiness of being*
— *Edward Hirsch*

Awake at 5 a.m. Crows make their crow noises. Other birds,
too loudly singing, are not beautiful. Pets, likewise, too early,
want to be fed, to pee.

All of this irritates me. The three-quarter moon — powdery
in the not-yet-sunlit sky —and I begin, pen in hand, less to claim
the day that has yet to begin, than to occupy myself away
from grouchiness.

Daybreak is a time for sound effects. Robins squeaking, all
kinds of birds, high and low, woodpeckers tap-tapping, high-
pitched insects, the scritch-scratch of this pen on the page.
The ducks squawk…the hen leads her brood to nibble
on the grass and will soon spoil it with their poop.

Deeper crow tones in the distant trees. Squirrels scrape
with their arguing.

As the hour opens toward more waking, sunlight softly
angles in and laurels, clover, lichens color things. The quilt
of rooflines threaded to the pines across the lake. A robin picks
at mites under its wing and a pink-breasted something or other
plucks fruits from the serviceberry tree.

A bundle of cosmic events, chemical reactions, my American
birth, bring me to this maple table with my steaming mug
in an encounter with all the goings on of this early day. I argue
with Hirsch's 'luckiness of being.' Let's just say that my arrival
here this morning, my reluctant attention, are an act of will.
Perhaps praise comes naturally from attention. Restored.
As easily accessible as turning my head, opening my eyes and ears.

Seems a truer thought than luck. Not simply being, but
making it count for something. I am alive.

Hymn for Naming the Difficult Times

—for Tim Flanagan

Season of hardship?
Season of light?

One flows from the other,
has always been like this, will
go this way again.

Soft souls are crying.
The hardest stones are crying, too — each
according to its own way.

So, then, sing *this* to the heavens,
sing to the pit:

Shake us up! Root our blindness out.
Our not-seeing, now is almost-nearly welded—neglect-stuck—
to the tender organs trying to bust out.

Pry that stuff from the part we were born with,
so it might unite with our aching hearts.

Prayer

—for Dana

An angel said, "Write your story,"
said it in that matter-of-fact way made famous
by the other angels: "Do not be afraid."

Do not be afraid to feel, timid rabbit,
stopped cold — frozen — as the bobcat lunges.

There were times, long-gone but neon-bright,
their grammar etched in cranial bone — petrified grooves —
through which all thought and feeling pass while still confined.

All of who I am equals a font of deflection, anything
to save myself from the worst of it — forever again.

Another angel said, "Can you take her hand
and bring her to that place behind your heart?"

What do I know of such a place?

God help me,
on my knees; my heart,
not a cell made of cinder block;
I fear my dwelling there.

35

Psalm: My De Profundis

Without willing it to happen
the mind, being not an organ but a phenomenon,
hijacks itself.

It works like this:
from the lakeside, painting the peeling slats of an old
    Adirondack chair
        with spring warblers and sunshine
        with Fauré through the headphones,

then walking on the gravel road to get the mail,
at the curve where the frogs mate in the spring pools,
whatever dreaming might have been
becomes wrenched by a memory that sinks in the gut-pit so quick.
Brought back five years to his telephone voice,
"I have relapsed again, shot heroin for the first time."

The image then (and now) made by those words,
more sickening than the most vile,
more frightful than a bad guy coming at me with a gun.

Such a short walk, such a quiet road.
It came from deep inside. The music did it.
Fauré's cello opened the vault.
Like the disciple, I am urged into deep water.
I want to be ready for this.

The Meeting Field: An Attempt to Conjure

1.

Thanksgiving morning — sky and lake, the same gunstock gray.
Trees — dark, vertical slices.
Small birds at the feeders, punctuation marks on a dull metal
plane...except —
    active, tracing dotted trails between freezing and survival.
The human families are shuttered to themselves, disrupted,
because of the virus,
    illness, disease, suicide, addiction. A relentless quotidian.
Disrupted.
The virus, an illness, a disease, a suicide, an addiction,
the relentless quotidian.

'...as if a gate had been left open in the usual life.'

Suffering ruptures a thin place,
tears the observable layer.
'As if a gate has been left open.'

What comes in? What goes out?

2.

Do I have such a gate, luring me toward an inner world
with all its tangles, where memories are manufactured and
embedded? Or does it point toward the outside, where events,

with all *their* tangles, occur; in "real time." A gate that confines
the "I," defines the "I," who pursues the passing? A passage
for the "I" to pursue?

See what I mean about tangles?

A passage into what I've come to know as the meeting field,
where the skin is an open membrane for exchange. Presenting
an exchange with the world. Boundaryless, open mesh, and
best entered through the heart's opening.

And in a dream the angel said, "Take yourself to that place
behind your heart."

I used to think my mind was limitless. Maybe it is; but either
way, it contains the rupture left by ideologies, attachments —
noise of hopes and wishes — which make an aloneness, the
plumb line, that arrow flight — meridian to the meeting field.

3.

That day, when I came upon the meeting field, I entered as
would Oppen's deer— 'bedded down, alien teeth tearing at
the grass, the roots of it dangle.' Two angels approached.
Faceless angels — I could tell from their light glow; they
carried a message I was meant to receive. I was not afraid
of their legless, wingless, robelessness. "Do not be afraid"
is the message angels usually begin with, but mine were
speechless. Their surprising likeness to a throbbing cosmic
sea — meaning: all the colorful nebulae you would expect and

galaxies and planetary systems heaving and swelling, atomic and tidal. And I was not afraid. We were together for some time and they reassured me that peace is a constant flow, born in the meeting field and borne out from there by me, should I choose. I distrusted them right away.

'You cannot carefully calculate and enter the unknown.' You cannot enter the meeting field except by jumping. The proverbial leap. Unlike Oppen's deer, no 'coming upon it' while shouldering the burdens of my beliefs, while lit by the hope of hope. No, something other: 'Make straight the way' — confession, repentance, forgiveness. Repentance, as in the ancient sense of, "to think anew."

4.

Witness — suffering that can't be stopped. Witness — suffering that can. Witness —the darkness; sometimes a permeable darkness. Witness — the feeble light. 'As if a gate has opened in the usual life.'

5.

And, angels are not always made of light. In the meeting field, you are more likely to encounter their darkness — vacant outlines, vacant faces, caverns where I am reminded: anything I do, think, say will be pulled by unfathomable dark matter toward irretrievable. It started, after all, with suffering. A virus. An Illness. A disease. A suicide. An addiction. Quotidian. Whatever lens I have ever used, clouded and rubbed clean by pain. A kind of dark light opposing light. In the absence of presence, I can almost see my wrong turns. And I can accede to the abyss. A kind of grace. Gravity and grace.

I can hold you with me in the meeting field. Accept your brokenness. I can blanket us with despair or hoist us with the thick rope of hope. Hope, which has no proof to prove its potency. Hope, which insists to the shipwreck: "No. No. Don't give up." Hope, the one verifiable energy that originates from nowhere known, but comes and throws its lifeline, strands of darkness, strands of light, woven tight. 'It's easy to say you believe a rope to be strong and sound as long as you are merely using it to cord a box.'

Here is: 'that which is.' Utterness. My own, all creatures', minerals', waters', stars': 'That they are there.' The utterness of my embeddedness in a torturous system where the only relief is acceptance of anxiety and grief. Immutable, they deceive; reliable, they come and go.

In unwalkable snow — gorgeous, thigh-high drifts — the stable place where boot meets earth gives way. I could fall. I could float in frozen cloud dust while the tiny birds succeed toward the feeders in the blizzard wind, their thin bare legs gain purchase on the perches and probe the bark's tiny openings for seed. Whether they like it or not.

6.

In the meeting field, the vast shadow of the known meets the
infinite fire of what can't ever be known. Meanings unmake
themselves. 'As if a gate has been left open in the usual life.'
Enter with caution, drop your knowledge and questioning
along the way, a weighted excess that never serves. Here, the
only tool I need is hope and "I don't know." With it, I can
draw belief from its cell, burrowed, submerged, sunk, deep in
the flesh cleft behind my heart. And the angel said, "Take her
to that place behind your heart."

*A different voice said, "Go out and stand on the mountain, a presence
is about to pass by."*

*Then a great and powerful wind tore the mountains apart and
shattered the rocks, but the voice was not in the wind. After the wind
there was an earthquake, but the voice was not in the earthquake.
After the earthquake came a fire, but there was no voice in the fire.
And after the fire came a gentle whisper. When I heard it, I pulled my
cloak over my face and went out and stood at the mouth of the cave.*

Then a voice said, "What are you doing here?"

7.

I say to myself: "A gate has opened, you may pass through.
Be tender with your fears, they can come, too." And in
the dimming light, the gate, unhinged, offered an opening,
beckoning,
a caution,
a threshold.
And the angel said, "Do not be afraid. Where you are; here
you can be."

8.

The meeting field is a mirror, we see ourselves as we actually
are: the cragged face of beleaguered, buried, baptized and
damned. "Remember you are dust and unto dust you shall
return."

The meeting field is *ignis fatuus,* will-o'-the-wisp, ghost light of
the dank swamp and the decomposed.

The meeting field is a remembered dining room where the
family gathers two times a year; when tempers flare, glasses fly
and all four children go underground, transfixed equally by the
awful sounds and the four wooden lion's paws, one for each of
us, veined in tensile anticipation.

The meeting field is a white surrender flag hanging in the limp
wind. Or a full-on battle flag, stiff in the attacking gust of
armor and gallop.

The meeting field is the snowy expanse of the iced-over lake. Red fox trotting on the cove after tearing apart a crow. Its signature — urine and scat — left among the ragged black feathers and bloody bones.

The meeting field is the least hospitable clearing...where flood-soaked furrows prevent all attempts toward hope's germination. And in the next season — scorched from too much heat, I might kick the dusty stubble or sink to my knees in muck. Trudge, give up, trudge again. I am Job's unidentified sister, by some miracle I see myself there. 'A gate...'

9.

What happens in the meeting field?

Where is it? Who arrives?

What is the child of that union?

A gate has opened in your usual life.
In my usual life.

Do I pass through the gate? Does Dickinson's 'feathered thing' pass through me? Does a great secret emerge from within me to merge with me? On some days in the meeting field, the 'thing that sat on Henry's heart' stands up and walks.

What remains?
A fleshy mess? A beautiful freedom?

Maybe it's the "no-matter-what" kind of love that everybody
      talks about.

Wilderness: Waking to What Is

1

Into the wilderness.
Land of hardship, land of dark learning.

Encamped. Ill-equipped to fathom, over-equipped to avoid.
Without landmarks — useless as "what was" or "what might be."
Land of "The way it is."

2

"Jesus was led by the Spirit into the wilderness."

Moses's people saw God there — somewhere between their
    slavery and his promise.

Our one true dwelling place — in the empty spaces
between maudlin, lament, and wishes.

3

You know Job's story. A swarm of ordeals.
His friends wage argument with his calamity,
urge him toward a hope he declines. "If God passed me,
I would not see him."

His friends, true to him, even within their bad news:
"So, you think your life is spotless, your conscience clear?"

Job grapples, Job defends. "But I am not an idiot."
We are like him, want to plead our case in God's court.

He knows God's in charge.
But Job has not yet woken to what is.

4

The wilderness is nearer than breath, than heartbeat, nearer
    than the next best thought.
One does not enter the wilderness; it descends, emerges, sidles up.
From the wilderness, I see with all the clarity I crave, with a
    dark clarity,
the 'inescapable brutality' of what is.

It might be birdsong after thin legs freeze to spring-iced branches.
It might be carcass at the edge of the drought-sunk water hole.
It might be a loved one perched on the bridge railing.

5

'The Spirit led Jesus into the wilderness.'
We are led to our separate reckonings, test after test.
We face them all.
Encamped, vigilant, weaned from our competencies.
If I suffer, it is because I have not trusted.

The inescapable brutality
'and on it your eye sets tearless,
and the dark is dear to you as the light.'

Prayer: Ripples

Oh Lord,
give me the soft ripples of lake water
as it fans out from the mallard's quiet paddling feet.
Afford me the shimmer and shake of its soft brokenness.
And the water's healing and re-healing. To become whole
    again
after splitting open, because if creation's pattern
is duplicated, then what I see on the lake
happens also in me and I am comforted.

He Must Have Trembled
— *after Caravaggio's* Doubting Thomas

Jesus must have been afraid.
He gripped the wrist of Thomas,
slid his finger far, all
into the wound, all
muscle and bone,
where it rested, a question
laid upon his heart, question
close, quick
upon his beating heart.

Jesus must have been afraid.
How he loved this man.

Some Things I Have Learned

There are parts within —
None are bad, none are good.

When parts — alone — speak their one word,
    it is made of two: me / you.
When parts cannot speak, but only show themselves —
    All are pure. Some, pure and terrifying darkness,
    Others pure and reassuring light.

When parts cannot speak, but only show themselves in unison —
    cosmic: bright stars that can't be seen without the darkness,
    darkness made more dark by the neighboring light.

If parts finally speak in unison —
the one word they utter, together,
is LOVE.

Homer's Whale

— for Homer Perkins, 1944–2014

My friend, booze-beaten, was cast into the roiling sea.
Before his liver failed him, the dark disease spit him out.
One last chance to get it right.

I don't think he thought too much about Jonah when he found
    the chunk of pine.
But, Homer carved a whale — chiseled, curved, sanded, oiled
    — and gave it to me.

It rests lightly; rocks in the breeze on my window sill, a marble
    for its eye.
The glass winks when the sun gleams through. When the
    storm clouds come, it glares sometimes, too.

I'd like to say I'm not like him, but that would be a lie. I've
    fled, connived,
blamed and bargained. Bankrupt in the gales of my own
    making.

Before his liver failed him, Homer made a whale.
He set a glass marble for its eye
and placed it in my hand.

On the Camping Road – Apex, North Carolina

Here I am, among the long-leaf pines
along with my body and my brain.
Together with sunshine and breezeshine and leafcrunch and
    mudslip
and the naked-necked death birds circling way up high.

Together, we make a mind whose project
is not conclusion, whose resting place
is movement, whose source is sourceless.

There are worries in the world
and I have plenty that seem "more than,"
of more severity than run-of-the-mill.

Out here, this larger mind of mine can handle it.
Or might be able to. Or so it seems,
which is fine with me,
with all of us, who together hike up and down, over and around.

Save me from myself, large mind, I pray.

To Gather My Desire into One Simple Word

1.

My heart reaches toward something I know.
Its unfound face, its shape : a nothing.

This nothing that I know : my hidden river, hollow, well, the wing.

I want to name it. You.

2.

Every name I say extends my hand:
You, The Well, My Hidden River . . .
Otherness, like distance, rises
like desire. Weight, a glance,
the thirsting of a river for its sea.

3.

I know a hollow where the river runs.
HaMakom, a Hebrew name for 'The Place,' metaphor for God.

I want to give God a name.

4.

In the unspoiled world of my imagining
you are the dove
and I am the hollow you soar above
or I rise

and you are the earth's musty closeness, a holy well.

I love your imagined hands.
Lake-like, you settle me, like summer.
Wild fruit, ripe like rain
about to fall but not yet falling.

You think yourself in me.
You are a river whose rapids sing in me.

Movement

is the one reliable thing.

And then it — also —

moves.

Lake Michigan, Early Morning, Late September

Dusty pastel, like one of Monet's cathedrals,
punctuated, surprising, by *kerruling* gulls
far from the sea.

Just east of the fallen city
just east of the rumbling belching fumes,
the lake looks Galilean.

A lone swimmer — wet-suited — raw skin shielded
from the bone-cutting cold. His radical actions,
diving into his smallness out there, at the edge.

If I could only jump and follow.
But, dressed for different work, shouldering a satchel of ideas,
I am due for a meeting soon. I am without his courage,
have not grown into my apostleship. Though I talk as if.

Dreaming on God's Stone

I want, need, want.
I trudge, wrestle, trip my way
into and through this puzzle.
Repentance arrives only when pushed to the brink.

One day I tripped on an acorn
      and fell asleep on a round stone.
Up through the moss, up from earth's thin rich brown,
      up through ancient layers, molten and granite-hard.
Up into my ear poured the many secrets of lightness
      and of dark.

And a voice said, "Tell your story."
And the same voice said, "Will be found."

From Within

— *after Simone Weil's* First and Last Notebooks

From within the egg
From within the egg of the world
From within the egg of the world I pierce the shell,
then I see the face of necessity . . .

Palm pressed
          from within the chalky shell;
from within,
            the faintest field of weakness,
            the inevitable peck, peck, peck;
and then the light, the bewildering light.

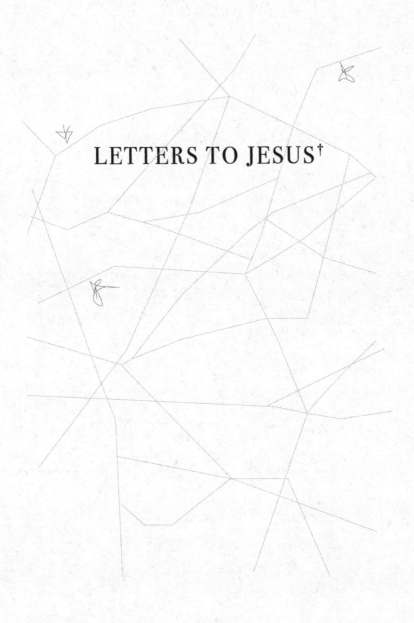

LETTERS TO JESUS†

Dear Jesus,

You come as presence.
You may have been with me always,
    but I did not know until now.

Why did you stay away? Why did you finally come,
    concealed in an odd voice while I emerged from a dream?

You echo Ezekiel, "I will trade your stone heart for my own."
Close, on one knee next to me, then gone.

[Ezek. 36:26–27]

Dear Jesus,

You asked your friends, "Who do you say I am?"

Well, to answer, I need to discover
whether what I know — or think I know — is mine.
Like St. John of the Cross, I face an 'impediment of ideas,'
my training has ruined me.

Even at my late age, I need to begin again.
For now, I must let go of your name. Forgive me,
you are diluted by too much of what others say.

[Matt. 16:15]

Dear Jesus,

What may I call you to make you new to me?
River. Wing. Deep Well? Too mystic.

How about "Hank?" Down-to-earth. Accessible.

How about "brother"? No, not holy enough.
How about "Holy Brother"? Familial, but not overly exalted;
    intimate,
but not romantic. Capitalized, to show your stature and my
    respect.

Let's try that.

Good morning, Holy Brother.

The sun is up; warblers offer God's evidence to the invisible air.

While walking with you through your father's fields and
    sidewalks,
my work is to cast off inherited stories and to imagine you.

Let us continue. Let us rest.
And I will attend to what you show me. I hope
it is your tenderness, as the priests have said.

Holy Brother,

at the sea's edge —
glittery sands, ground glacial rocks. And human imprints —
not yours at Capernaum, but I imagine so.

Which leads to you, here with me. Beautiful!
Your love stories, subversive!
I am barefoot here, available
for you to radicalize me!

Holy Brother,

everyone knows your face
and no one knows for sure; so,
you can have any face, brother —
angry scowl at the temple
soft eyelids at the well
sunlit glorious eyebrows raised to heaven on the God-bathed
    mountain.

I've always wondered —
what did your face say when you
turned your back on the angry crowd,
the crowd about to stone the woman to death?

What did your face say when you wrote that thing in the sand?

[Matt. 21:2–17, John 4:7–26, Matt. 17:2, John 8:1–11]

Tender Brother,

give me the grace to not be pious when I think of you,
to be as earthy as a donkey's rump or a maggot's rotted food.
The robes in Rome must have gotten it wrong —
all you wanted was to feed the crowds.
You would have liked the dice they threw for your clothes.

Forgive me for talking to you this way.
Walk on water, if that's the kind of thing you like to do. Turn
   it into wine.
Just don't expect me to get all highfalutin about it when you
   reach out so tenderly,
though I may get misty-eyed.

My Holy Brother,

I sit here under the crooked oak.
Is it shade or shadow that covers me?
Storm-cracked, breeze-danced — it could go either way. And has.
If you would sit with me here, our boney backs against
    the bark ridges,
the curved trunk, shoulder to shoulder, you might pass to me
    your calm dignity.

And you said, *Don't be afraid. Keep awake.*
Love God. Love even the troublesome ones.
Forget your objects of hate or infatuation.

Oh wow. To BE with you!

[Matt. 28:10; Lk. 12:32; Mk. 14:38]

Oh, my Holy Brother

"Bear your cross."
"Leave all you know behind."

Difficult brother,
Your demands tase me.

Holy Brother,

As much as I pray, I do so from the safety of mind.
Is it a failure to say, I have not yet *felt* your love?
I have not yet knelt in the fire that burns for you.
My boat may have set out into deep waters — but I have not
    dived down.

Draw me into the dark, dear Brother. Your sea beckons me.
Transform me there from mild to fierce with love for you.

[Rom. 8:26–27]
[Lk. 5:4]

Holy Brother,

You ask me to burn my bucket-full of riches, my wounds,
which I also hoard, despite my cluttered basement, my
  pummeled soul.

Burn the pile, but I resist, not sure who I would be
without their chaos, knit into me.

Find me, Holy Brother.

I am as near to you as I have ever been.

Holy Brother,

My heart beats, fist-sized organ pumps, not granite —
but garnet/jewel wine blood.

Our hearts look at each other, portals,
optic cords through which sight is made more sure.

Yours: open sacred.
Mine: flames out of its bone cage.

Good morning, Holy Brother.

The Church says today is Ash Wednesday, the first day of Lent,
a season of repentance and pleas. Come closer, Brother.
Come with me into my room. Can you be with me after I shut
    the door?
Teach me to pray the way you do, aware of Moses's laws, but
    free from them too.
I know you will say, "Do not be afraid." "Abide in me as I
    abide in you."
OK. I understand; the room is mine alone. *I* built its
    hodgepodge, rickety, worm-holed walls.
I feel your hand on my shoulder, the warm thread lighting my
    heart.
You help me push the rusted hinges. One step — into the
    cluttered corners.

May I have your stamina and fierce tenderness — Holy Brother,
help me to learn what I need to know.

[Matt. 28:10; Lk. 12:32; Mk. 14:38; John 15:4]

Dear Holy Brother,

I wake this morning content with health and time.
Though I suffer my small indignities and wounds,
I am rich. Though I have been an agent of pain for others
and suffer my guilt and remorse, I am wealthy. But my focus is
    monocular.

When I say "I," where is the storekeeper with rotted teeth?
The drunk addict slumping in the urine-soaked alley?
The belly-bloated children or the ones with belt-scars on their
    bottoms?
Where are the watery creatures choking on our junk?

I know you mean for me to be in them, too...
to bear their sufferings as I do mine. To make theirs mine.
Why, if you want this, does it not come naturally? Why don't I
live *their* lives as naturally as I do "my own"? God separated us
and then urges us back together, back toward you.
That's weird and almost sadistic, sorry to say.

Good morning, Holy Brother.

I have felt you with me each day these last months. I HAVE
read your Gospels. Does this please you? Is my pleasing you
something that pleases you? And you then say to me in a
dream, "I want you to say something about the beautiful."
Wow, I am like Ezekiel — fed the words I need to say. But,
Lord, I see so much; the abundance pours forth — and that's
not hyperbole. It's actually raining hard at the moment in
Georgia's piney woods where we are camped among the gnats
so small they pop through the screens and into my nose when
I breathe. And their bites are as hard as a horse's, 10,000 times
their size. But owls hoot and doves coo and my lover snores in
the candlelight by which I ask for you and you arrive.

[Ezek. 2:1–3:3]

My dear Brother,

I am glad you are here with me in my shame as I read John's
Gospel about the adulterous woman. I will always wonder
what I would have done if I had known you then like I know
you now. I was "out of my depth," responded to my passions
without temperance.

Thank you, thank you — uncontainable Christ — for your
reminder,

"Those without sin, cast the first stone." But, you haven't
answered yet. What *did* you write in the sand that day? Your
thoughts and God's mercy etched with a human hand on that
changeable page? Were you doodling, like a brilliant but bored
youth, unmoved by the elders' babble? Were you writing to
God, asking for guidance? I think you were writing to me,
sitting here in my sinner's room, 2000 years in the future. *Put
down your stones. Here is my heart, on fire for you, so you might have
light to see.*

[Jn 8:53]

Good morning, Holy Brother,

This week the Christian world will reenact your torture, will remind itself of the strength of your faith while you were dragged through the dregs of human arrogance. I want so much to be with you, really *with* you, unmediated.

What do you want me to know about you? I am waiting for you to say something cryptic, or tell a slanted story about a vine or tree. Please don't turn your back. Or throw it back to me, "Who do you say I am?" I am schooled in your trajectory: sent, brought forth, demonstrated, ministered, healed, conveyed, tortured, killed, raised. How am I to grasp an inhuman, ungraspable infinity? The kingdom you died for, and because of, resembles no earthly place. I only have this one unfortunate power: projection of human ways, which falls as short as a snapshot.

Such small concepts, such small feelings. And so, here I sit, an hour into this unsent letter, trusting each pen stroke, each hesitation, each distraction, each need to pee; trusting my query will reach you. Sitting here with Lazarus, Martha and Mary and that awful Judas. Please let all of this be as Mary's nard.

How did you do it? You knew you were God's scapegoat. And you are my concrete unfathomable who says only, *LOVE.*

[Matt. 16:13–20, John 12:1–8]

Holy Brother,

I am deep in seclusion this morning. Today's Gospel yet
    unopened.
Trying to imagine you. You, free of the Euro/Aryan pictures
    I've been encircled by.
Show me your brown eyes, your Jewish skin. Come to me,
    here, please.
Come to me across the immeasurable distance between us, my
    deepest water.

Holy Brother,

Help me to understand your last meal —
your knowing and moving through the pre-ordained
while those who loved you either tried to hold you back,
tethered you to their own needs and fears,
or took advantage of the opportunity of your destiny to cash in.
Your best friend leaned against your chest to hear you predict
    the betrayal.
The closeness of that! How I imagine that closeness would feel,
    your beating heart
on my cheek and ear, at once comforting and lonely.
Betrayal is lonely.
If I am, in reality, as close to you as I feel now — help me to
    accept your mystery.

Holy Brother,

Easter has come and gone. I am back to my pondering.

I am reading ideas of Jewish rabbis. One said in a letter to a student, God created the world because it is in God's nature to manifest wholeness and possibility, that — as with a magnet, which cannot be itself without its two opposing poles — this earthly troubled world and God's eternal Godness are one. God's timeless cycle of inhalation and exhalation exploding itself into itself over and over inside and outside of all histories, inclusive of all the honored particulars.

But what about me? Earthly bundle of petty and cosmic concerns, thimble-sized delights and unholdable fears, spontaneously created and creating until my time runs out. I can feel the pull toward God, and I can feel the drift and sprint away. That's the point, right? To accept the drift but to give in to the pull. Witness and testify through my one reliable action — Praise.

Good morning, my Holy Brother.

This week has overwhelmed me.
I do not feel the release, the joy of your rising.
I wonder who to pray to? God? You? The Holy Spirit? Your
mother? My saints and angels? All of creation? So I sit in
silence or do my chores and let it all wash over me.
It's too much, and is supposed to be.

Einstein said, "If I had an hour to solve a problem and my life
    depended on the solution,
I would spend the first 55 minutes determining the proper
    question to ask."

Oh, Holy Brother,

whose sacred heart fires me and the world, give me the
    courage to ask the question:
"What do you want of me?"

And then — in a dream — you gave me this image: *Take the
five threads you have been given. Weave them into Creation's ever-
forming mesh...extend it, deepen it, make it stronger...connect your
threads to others, add energy and "reach."*

Oh Jesus, I have no idea what you mean. What are the
    threads? Where are they hidden?
Are they hidden? My hands are empty, and I am all thumbs.

A Dialogue

What does love ask of me?
Radical acceptance,
commitment to engagement and reconciliation.

How is it put into practice?
When confronted with anger, aggression, insults, ask yourself,
'What am I afraid of?'
Move into my deepest heart, where God's affirmation will meet you.

Holy Brother, Maybe I cannot know what Divine love is like,
even though I think about it all day long. If I close my eyes and wait
for you to show me, these are the images that arrive: warmth, light.
Love beams to me, like sunshine absorbed by the fern
and reflected back in the water droplet let go in its evening breath.

Who is saying these words? I do not recognize myself
and yet I know I have been this person from the start.
The smudges on the mirror you have been using are rubbed cleaned now.
We have put a new one in your hand.

You are raised outside of time. Flame of my heart,
help me not to see you, but to see *with* you, *because* of you.

RAISING THE SPARKS‡

‡ *See the Notes*

The Light, the Vessels, the Shards: Raising the Sparks

Today, my boot slipped on a rock and sank ankle-deep.
The frigid spring creek seeped between my wool-covered toes.
I didn't say a word out loud, but inside: "Damn it!"
And then — graced — a memory, a rabbi's story:
"The world is filled with sparkling shards — moss,
the stream, my boot and socks and toes. Even
my teeth, my tongue positioned behind my
teeth in order to make my "Damn!"
Even the "Damn" — the idea and the feeling together —
their anger and impatience and grief for
having to slog home with one foot aching cold.
All of them sparkling with God light.

Can you believe it?
God, so long ago, exhaled stuff so huge,
it broke the vessels and scattered their shards. The rabbi said I am
to notice and gather and raise those shards, to bring them into
a circle of repair, a circle of the world's repair.

Damn! Can you see the word's sparkle? Shining here from
within this poem? Read the word out loud, read it while thinking
about the rabbi's story. When you say it, you will join the circle
made by all the noticing and gathering and raising. And we will
be whole again in our suffering, astonishment and our praise.

My List of Sparks

Sitting in my morning chair, thinking about God's sparks.

Where have I noticed them? Where might they be dormant,
        waiting to be raised?
What's left of last night's surprising April snow
        flattened metallic reflections on the overcast lake,
November's acorns bursting now, their rosy shoots packed
        and poised to transform the sunshine to towering oak.
My heart beats in familiar iambs, my lungs inflate, bunions ache,
        arthritic thumbs fumble with an ink-filled pen.
Someone invented ultra-violet decals to warn the birds
        about the glass.
                And birds — in the first place — fly. And hang and swim
                and build homes with their mouths and tiny wood duck
                chicks jump from tall trees without dying and
                woodpeckers — with air pockets between their bones —
                hammer impossible trees without cracking their skulls.

And that's an infinitesimal fraction that can be multiplied by
   7 million species of earth's animals and plants, which equals —
   What?! And who knows about the minerals, gases, deep-water beings
   neither plant nor animal nor mineral.
Or the sparks sheltering far off in the future somewhere.
Not to mention those embedded in Tolstoy's miraculous sentences.
Not to mention the coyote running free on Chicago's Michigan
Avenue on a day a virus forced folks like me to give up the streets.

Where are the Sparks in the Messes I Make?

This is the crucible where the soul meets the heat that purifies,
that burns off the useless that once was useful, essential but

useful no more. Here it goes — smoke to sky and ash to earth
leaving the basic one thing, the first seed around which

the now-dry husk hides and hid
the ever-creating collaborating single core.

This God-logic makes no sense. This burning,
uninvited, required so the heart might birth again and again.

Where Are the Sparks in a Cotton Field?

Out in the Carolinas, way west
of any metropolis or ocean condo lot,
the land puffs as far as you can see with dry stems and fluff balls.
Picking season, yet to come; fields unworked, for now.
And we park alongside a ditch to touch. You say,
"Have you ever felt it raw?"
Dressed from head to toe in some fancy version of the stuff,
I say: "Let's go."

The tiny clouds sit prickly in their husk; knuckle scrapes
remind us of "American" slaves forced to pick
the seeds buried deep in some ungodly trinity: the master's grail,
the worker's unnatural burden, the plant —
just being itself in the suffering heat.

I tucked a bunch in a Ziploc bag, to put on my bedtime shelf at home
so I'd never forget,
when sleeping deep in my 300-thread count sheets,
the scarred black hands that made it so.

Where Are the Sparks in Bitter Cold?

God, if you were here with me, I'd complain
about how near impossible it is,
all clenched from head to toe,
no matter all the sloganed, hi-tech fabrics — "smart" this,
    "smart" that —
designed by some whiz-bang kids to do some good
(and make some dough).

How the mind gets triggered to shiver,
to fight to stay alive even though
the hearth burns within easy reach.

And get a load of this, even in your absence —
an insight managed to muscle in:
the heart doesn't much like whining
and its embers take the wee-est bit of fanning to flame.

Raising the Sparks from the Flood-Stained Waters

A big storm sent the hair-slivered creeks downstream fast

to join the greater ones to add
their flowing bounty to the lesser rivers,
which offer their swell to the too-high
too fast, snag-hiding, limb-carrying Suwannee,

By the time the swallowing waters gained
on Mexico's Gulf, every spring run and low land in its path
swelled and roiled; "normal" was gobbled up
by the simple rain's sometimes greed.
Everything suffers: banks slide and tree roots
dangle without their grounding soil, mostly washed away.
The locals call it a "normal ruin." It happens: the sky
turns bad and cracks and rumbles. The sign post in the park
where I stand marks the high points. The highest
would have killed me, two feet over my head.

That's the way it went, the way it goes — fresh to salt,
then heated to rise and fall again. They say it will
get worse. More and worse. Today, the ancient cypress
wear an unnatural, natural set of banded yellow marks
where high water was once and will be, reliably, again.

Sparks/Surprise: Adel, Georgia

Mild
Mild breeze, mild birds, mild April leaves, newly unfurled.
Mild live oak tree making mild shade.
Mild mannered people and
Spanish moss — mild, in the breeze, like lacy scarves on a
     dancer's limbs.

Good to have "mild" after so much crisis.
Good to feel "soft" after feeling so clenched.

And in the midst, a blue-backed bird with a chestnut chest —
     the surprise
it fostered by lifting up unexpectedly as we passed, engaged
with our habitual looking in the other direction, then "caught"
by its flash and flittery flight.

It's a good expression, isn't it: "Caught by surprise." We, who
     strive so mightily to be free,
wrestle with our containment, whose problems are never truly
     solved by anything planned for or known — as in the way,
     if seeing a vulnerable wildflower on the trail, everyone
     wants to know its name. "Wild gentian." "Oh," someone
     says; all the energy thereby sucked from the encounter.

If I bend down, instead, and invite them to feel the soft-fuzzed
   stem, the "catch" is in.
Kneeling, smiling, feeling the plant's surprise — we stay
   together — plant and people, for a long time.

I have been busy for many months with "figuring out,"
   searching the various definitions.
At a loss to explain, unable to be mild.

How rarely do I offer myself to be caught.

Raising the Sparks by Going against My Grain

Since I was a child I've been enamored with matters of scale,
preoccupied with whether the trickle of water on the beach
looks to an ant as the breaking wave
looks to me. Whether the picnic under my umbrella
reproduces itself like images in back-to-back mirrors
by families everywhere on the big round earth. When digging
a much deeper hole than was needed for the castle's moat,
it surely seemed, as the grown-ups said — that China was close.

Today, I learned the big picture isn't always the place to look.
While daydreaming about whether mom and dad might not
have known: longitude and latitude prove it wasn't China
but a place that hadn't become a country yet (Kyrgystan!),
I missed a tiny tick embedded in my partner's back. A day
earlier, trying to track the pelican squadron over the marsh,
a delicate clam shell crushed under my shifting boot.
Look close, look far, stay awake. That's what the good book says.

Aubade: Raising the Sparks from Under

The little chill of cloudless autumn mornings
leads me, circumspect, toward wonderment.
Light slants into the room's corners, into its underneaths
where tangles confine themselves, contain the scraps
kicked out of sight's way...but not, not really.
Hard to hang onto that — the way, if a ball rolls behind the bed,
a toddler believes it's gone for good.

This lowering sun offers diagonal sight lines
to the furniture's shadowed underside. What are those
silvery flecks of who knows what?
Hands and knees required to know — the palm-sized ball of
cobweb, cat hair, rug wool and an odd glitter there.

Raising the Sparks by Loving the Unlovable

Fred works with a toothless man
at a beat-up trailer in his yard
on a back road in Waycross, Georgia.
Don't take your camper's propane tank
to him for repair, even if he tells you
with confidence that it's probably
the regulator, "Regulators always
go first on those things." Yet, it might be
worth a trip just to meet him.
He'll surprise you with
a joke about the president and anyone
who "Has it made," which is really
directed at you because you're
on vacation and not working.
Even though he makes you laugh,
he'll try to charge you more than
you should pay for something
you can fix yourself…which you
couldn't have known without
the help of his toothless son,
who'll stick with you to troubleshoot
until you both discover the fault
is with the valve, which Walmart will
replace for free, even though Fred —
rummaging in his rusted hut of an office —
yells back "They ain't gonna take it back"

at the same time the Walmart guy on the
other end of the line says, "Sure.
Bring it in." You gotta love a guy
like Fred, out there in the swampy backwoods,
trying to make a buck with a son whose
generosity doesn't help. Not one bit.

Raising the Sparks from Human Lights

In dark morning, human lights are stars,
glowing streaks of gold and silver.

Tires swish on wet pavement,
crickets hum and chirp.

Early morning walkers cough below my window,
TV towers across town blink their warnings to the planes.

"Who cares?" says the cynic in me.
But that part can't see a thing, turned the other way, forever
    blustering and blubbering.

The Russian poet said we can't say anything about God but we
    can say everything to God.
We've lost our conscience and courage, busy explaining and
    justifying ourselves.

A little boy, Juan D., writes to God, "I want to trust you...I
    want you to help me to do it. Amen."

I want to, too. Something tells me to keep looking, look out at
    these invented lights.
They ruin the darkness. These mechanical gorgeous diamonds.

Oh God, is that you?

Raising the Sparks from Other People's Shoes

I have walked around today in a week filled with "without,"
surrounded by quotidian ordinary: my same old cell phone,
a smudged pair of glasses — hair tangled in the hinge. I am
    wondering
about the limitations of singular vision, trying, I swear,
to fulfill my mystical purpose…to discover something, anything,
about any old thing. But I'll bet you can fill in the blanks about
    how that goes.

And then, I am asked by Ignatius to put myself in Lazarus's shoes.
What does it feel like? Crumpled at the rich man's gate?
Nothing to eat. "The dogs lick your sores." Lazarus, they say
you are in heaven, circled in Abraham's arms. Come to me,
Lazarus; come, Rich Man, too. Together we'll repair the world.

What Kind of Sparks?

What kind of sparks can be raised from a mutating virus
against which a person can only keep her distance, wash her
   hands for 20 seconds
accompanied by the Lord's Prayer to mark the time?

Maybe this: we didn't know until too late how threaded
to each other we are.

Raising the Sparks from Clouds

Wishing for a more holy life, here
rests my urge. Nothing as grand as a public ministry,
more Mertonesque. Hermitage —
paper and pen; in the act of pressing
ink to page, grace would flow freely.

And I would, to clear my head-on-fire doing God's good work,
walk occasionally out the door, onto
the porch in a brisk or sultry air.
where I would be overcome
by the intricate order and surprise of clouds.

Here's what they told me: *We are like you: in formation,*
evidence of earth turning, breathing.
You can rely on us: there not there.

And so I ask, with this sort of sharing between me and clouds,
paper and ink, "What sort of thing is God?"

I have submitted. I have been led to this.

NOTES

LAMENTS AND BENEDICTIONS

To All of You, Who Are Out There

imagines the jeweled net of Indra, the Vedic deva. The
jewel connects multiple jewels and each jewel contains the
image of all the other jewels.

The Man Billions Pray With

includes a reference to T.S. Eliot's phrase "still point of the
turning world," from "Burnt Notion" in the *Four Quartets.*

In Dark Winter

the meter here approximates Anglo-Saxon stresses and
rhythms; "in the maker's holy hands" is from *Beowulf.*

Paradox

after a sculpture by Scottish artist Steve Dilworth.

Light Litany

contains a reference to Leonard Cohen's song "Anthem;"
"Long loving look at the real" is from Jesuit theologian
Walter Burghardt.

Bad Times and Their Causes

this title quotes nineteenth-century Artic balloonist S. A.
Andrée in *The Ice Balloon*, Alec Wilkinson (2012*).*

Meditation on a Photograph of a Manta Ray

refers to a series of photographs by Baltimore artist Jann Rosen-Queralt.

Body of Water

'A medium for an anemone to dream' is from one of George Oppen's "Daybooks (II-III)" in George Oppen's *Selected Prose, Daybooks and Papers*.

Snowed in

and *There is another world, and it is under this one*

reference a line from the writings of French poet Paul Éluard.

On Occasion of the Pittsburgh Synagogue Massacre

references lines from poets Paul Celan ("Death Fugue"), Osip Mandelstam (from Christian Wiman's 2012 translation, *Stolen Air*), and Yehuda Amichai ("Summer Evening at the Window with Psalms").

Praise restores us to the world again, to our luckiness of being

takes its title from Edward Hirsch's essay on Gerard Manley Hopkins in the anthology *Poet's Choice*.

Psalm: My De Profundis

responds to Psalm 130 and contains a reference to Luke's Gospel, 5:4.

The Meeting Field: An Attempt to Conjure

— '...as if a gate had been left open in the usual life' is from Seamus Heaney's "Found Prose."

— "Do not be afraid." This phrase appears multiple times in the New Testament Gospels.

— 'You cannot carefully calculate and enter the unknown.' From Jiddu Krishnamurti's *The Book of Life*.

— "Make straight the way," from the Gospel according to John 1:23.

— Repentance as in the ancient sense of: "to think anew;" to think beyond the way we think now, to turn around and think in a different way (Fr. Michael Kelly, SJ).

— 'a permeable darkness,' a phrase used by poet Anita Burrows to describe her depression.

— 'Gravity and grace,' is from Simone Weil's book of the same title.

— 'It's easy to say you believe a rope to be strong and sound as long as you are merely using it to cord a box' is from C. S. Lewis, *A Grief Observed*.

— 'That which is' and 'That they are there' are from George Oppen's poem "Psalm."

— The notion of cleft is from Exodus 33:22.

— *a voice said*, an adaptation from 1 Kings 19:11–13.

— Dickinson's 'feathered thing' refers to her poem 314 that opens with: "Hope is the thing with feathers— That perches in the soul—"

— 'The thing that sat on Henry's heart' is from John Berryman's *Dream Songs* (29).

— "Remember you are dust and unto dust you shall return," are words spoken by the priest on Ash Wednesday as the ashes are placed on the forehead.

Wilderness: Waking to What is

"Jesus was led by the Spirit into the wilderness" comes from Matthew's Gospel, 4:1; quotations from the *Book of Job* come from *Book of Job*, trans. Stephen Mitchell (New York: Harper Perennial, 1994). The phrase 'inescapable brutality' comes from Carol Muske-Dukes. *Los Angeles Review of Books,* December 4 2019, https://lareviewofbooks.org/article/and-then-music-on-the-collected-work-of-the-late-jane-mead/. Final stanza quotes both Muske-Dukes and Welsh poet R. S. Thomas. "Because," *Collected poems 1945-1990* (London: Orion Books, Ltd. 2000).

To Gather My Desire into One Simple Word

contains a variation on Paul Cézanne's statement "The landscape thinks itself in me."

Dreaming on God's Stone

was inspired by the story of Jacob's pillow. Genesis 28:11.

From Within

riffs with lines from Simone Weil, *First and Last Notebooks: Supernatural Knowledge,* trans. Richard Rees (Eugene, OR: Wipf & Stock, 2015).

Prayer
is inspired by a talk given by Franciscan sister Ilia Delio
and the work of the Center for Christogenesis. "Channel
of peace" comes from "The Prayer of St. Francis."

LETTERS TO JESUS

The letters in this section are part of my encounter, in
2018, with the sixteenth-century *Spiritual Exercises of
Ignatius of Loyola*. Written in 1548, the exercises are a
collection of meditations, prayers, and contemplative
practices developed by St. Ignatius to help people deepen
their relationship with God.

Early in Ignatius's *Spiritual Exercises*, we are asked to
meditate on Matthew's Gospel passage in which Jesus asks
Peter, "Who do you say I am?" (Matt. 16:13–19). Jesus is
asking us this question also.

St. Ignatius offers a few methods for approaching
this. He suggests a colloquy, an intimate conversation
with God, Jesus, Mary, or one of the saints (as a friend
speaking to a friend or as if to another whom one has
offended). These "Letters to Jesus" are my colloquies. The
section concludes with a dialogue between me and Jesus.
The biblical references at the end of some letters point to
particular passages from which a particular letter emerged.

RAISING THE SPARKS

Sixteenth-century mystical Judaism (Lurianiac Kabbalah)
presents a compelling idea of our purpose here on earth:
the concept of *tikkun olam*, or restoring divine perfection/
repairing the world. This notion derives from a sacred
story that recounts the "shattering of vessels," a suggestion
that at the beginning of time, God's presence filled the
universe. To make room for creation, God drew a breath
and contracted himself; first darkness and then, "Let there
be light." Ten holy vessels, filled with primordial light,
could not contain God's divinity. Some vessels shattered,
scattering shards invested with holy sparks throughout
creation. It was believed that, if people worked to "gather
or raise the sparks," then the vessels would be restored
and the repair of the world from its initial splitting would
be complete (*tikkun olam*). An implication of this belief
is that it is the duty of each one of us to raise the sparks
from wherever they are imprisoned and to elevate them
to holiness. The poems in this section are my imagining
of where and how these divine sparks might appear to me
and how I — through my actions and words — might raise
them.

Several books and articles noted in the citations
offer broader context for *tikkun olam* and contemporary
theological critiques of the concept.

Raising the Sparks by Going against My Grain
    there are multiple passages in the New Testament where
    Jesus asked the apostles to "stay awake."

Raising the Sparks from Other People's Shoes
    references St. Ignatius of Loyola's method of imaginative
    prayer, in which one imagines — in full sensory detail —
    being in particular biblical scenes. This poem imagines
    Luke's parable of Lazarus and the Rich Man, Luke
    16:19–31.

Raising the Sparks from Human Lights
    refers to Russian poet Marina Tsvetaeva and is inspired by
    her poem "God (3)."

CITATIONS

Carol Muske-Dukes. *Los Angeles Review of Books,* December 4, 2019. https://lareviewofbooks.org/article/and-then-music-on -the-collected-work-of-the-late-jane-mead/

Jill Jacobs. "History of 'Tikkun Olam'," *Zeek: Social Justice. Jewish. Catalyst. Community.* http://www.zeek.net/706tohu/ index.php?page=2

K. Kavanaugh & Otilio Rodriguez, eds. "Exposition on The Dark Night," Chapter 10, *Collected Works of St. John of the Cross* (Washington, DC: ICS Publications, 1991, 2017).

Stephen Mitchell, trans. *Book of Job* (New York: Harper Perennial, 1994).

Howard Schwartz. "How Ari Created a Myth and Transformed Judaism," *Tikkun: to heal, repair, and transform the world.* 2011. https://www.tikkun.org/how-the-ari-created-a -myth-and-transformed-judaism/

Rabbi Jeremy Schwartz. "Tikkun Olam, Unpacked." *Reconstructing Judaism,* 2016. www.reconstructingjudaism.org/ article/tikkun-olam-unpacked

Rami Shapiro, trans. *Open Secrets: The Letters of Reb Yerachmiel Ben Yisrael* (Rhinebeck, NY: Monkfish Book Publishing, 2004).

R.S. Thomas. "Because," *Collected poems 1945-1990* (London: Orion Books, Ltd., 2000).

Marina Tsvetaeva. "God (3)," translated by Paul Graves, in *Women in Praise of the Sacred: 43 Centuries of Spiritual Poetry by Women,* ed. Jane Hirshfield (New York: Harper Perennial; 1st edition, 1995).

Simone Weil. *First and Last Notebooks: Supernatural Knowledge,* trans. Richard Rees (Eugene, OR: Wipf & Stock, 2015).

ACKNOWLEDGMENTS

Many thanks to all those who have read these poems in various versions and who have guided me in my wonderings. Especially, Linda Bills, Mark Burrows, Philip Carr-Harris, Suzanne Garrigues, Rabbi Sam Gordon, Gonzaga Eastern Point Retreat House, Barbara Mahany, Paul Mariani, all the angels at Paraclete Press, Sherry Paulson, Dana Rosenstein Michael Salcman, Rabbi Rami Shapiro, and Father Dominic Totoro. My sons, Brian and Daniel Wallace, are my inspiration. This book is dedicated with love and gratitude to Judy Remmel, the one whose prayer parallels my own.

PREVIOUSLY PUBLISHED

"In Dark Winter" was included in 2017 exhibition of photographs/prints by Katherine Kavanaugh.

"Meditation on a Photograph of a Manta Ray"
Full Bleed: A Journal of Art and Design

"From Within"
Desire Path, Toadlily Press

"Hymn for Difficult Times"
Spiritus

"Prayer: Ripples"
Ekstasis Magazine

ABOUT THE AUTHOR

JENNIFER WALLACE lives in Shutesbury, Massachusetts. Her poems, essays, and photographs have appeared in artists books, exhibition catalogs, galleries, museums, anthologies, and literary journals. *Raising the Sparks* is her sixth poetry collection.

IRON
PEN

"O that my words were written down!
O that they were inscribed in a book!
O that with an iron pen and with lead
they were engraved on a rock forever!"
—*Job 19:23-24*

Outcast and utterly alone, Job pours out his anguish to his Maker. From the depths of his pain, he reveals a trust in God's goodness that is stronger than his despair, giving humanity some of the most beautiful and poetic verses of all time. Paraclete's Iron Pen imprint is inspired by this spirit of unvarnished honesty and tenacious hope.

OTHER IRON PEN BOOKS

Almost Entirely, Jennifer Wallace

Astonishments, Anna Kamieńska

The Consequence of Moonlight, Sofia Starnes

Eye of the Beholder, Luci Shaw

Glory in the Margins, Nikki Grimes

Idiot Psalms, Scott Cairns

Still Pilgrim, Angela Alaimo O'Donnell

To Shatter Glass, Sister Sharon Hunter, CJ

Wing Over Wing, Julie Cadwallader Staub

ABOUT PARACLETE PRESS

PARACLETE PRESS is the publishing arm
of the Cape Cod Benedictine community,
the Community of Jesus. Presenting a full
expression of Christian belief and practice,
we reflect the ecumenical charism of the
Community and its dedication to sacred
music, the fine arts, and the written word.

SCAN
TO
READ
MORE

Learn more about us at our website:

www.paracletepress.com

or phone us toll-free at 1.800.451.5006

You may also be interested in...

Almost Entirely
Poems

Jennifer Wallace

ISBN 978-1-61261-859-3 | $19 | 128 pages

Rooted in the grit of urban Baltimore and the forests of rural Massachusetts, these poems remind us that life's tensions and polarities are energies we carry within ourselves. These are poems of witness and commentary, conversation, and meditation. They offer moments of close looking, and of looking away; of loving, and of bungled attempts to be more loving. They call us to look long and hard—and generously—at our lives. Written with radiant honesty and fierce tenderness, they suggest a path of inner discovery where mystery awaits us in the ordinary.

"Wallace's new collection is a stark book: sincere in its continual engagement with doubt, silence, absence, and loneliness. The author concedes in her epigraph that she struggles to reconcile faith and her 'Western mind'; her Triton, rather like Wordsworth's, is to 'deliver us from our unbelief.' Her God, a post-Kierkegaardian challenge, stimulates both a poetry and a faith in her that is 'a dense hollowness,' the only respites seeming to come from friendship, love, and natural scenes, vividly and respectfully glimpsed. Direct and heartbreaking." —*Library Journal*

Available wherever books are sold.
Paraclete Press | 1-800-451-5006 | www.paracletepress.com